BLAST OFF TO EARTH!

A LOOK AT GEOGRAPHY

FIELD TRIP →

BLAST OFF TO EARTH!
A LOOK AT GEOGRAPHY

WRITTEN AND ILLUSTRATED BY
LOREEN LEEDY

HARCOURT BRACE & COMPANY
Orlando Atlanta Austin Boston San Francisco Chicago Dallas New York
Toronto London

Go home, Woofer!

Woof!

TO VICKI

This edition is published by special arrangement with
Holiday House, Inc.

Grateful acknowledgment is made to Holiday House, Inc.
for permission to reprint *Blast Off To Earth! A Look At
Geography* by Loreen Leedy. Copyright © 1992 by Loreen
Leedy.

Printed in the United States of America

ISBN 0-15-302171-3

3 4 5 6 7 8 9 10   035   97 96 95 94

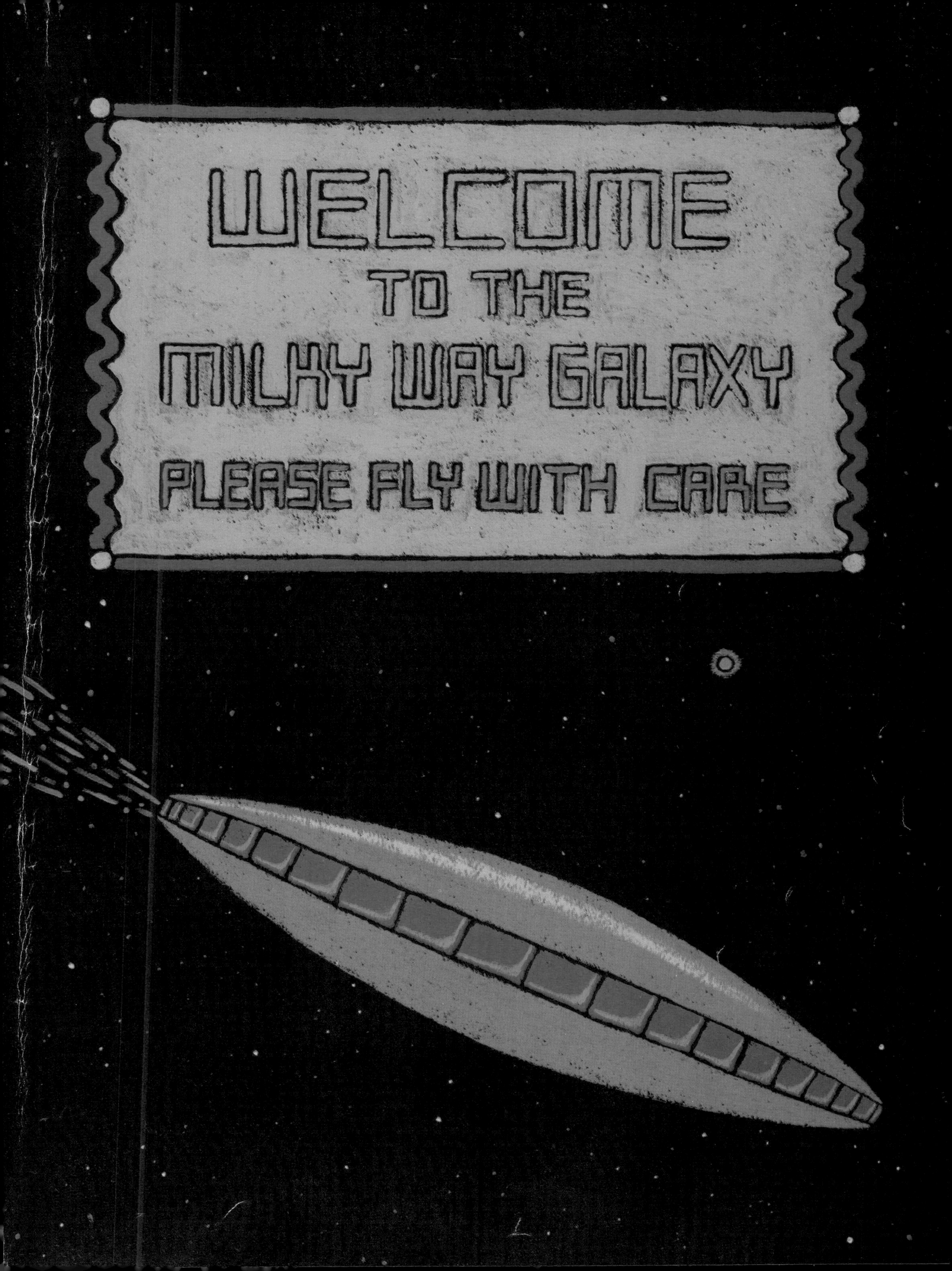
WELCOME
TO THE
MILKY WAY GALAXY
PLEASE FLY WITH CARE

How long till we get there, Mr. Quark?
Just a few more nanoseconds.
I have visual contact! It looks like a big, blue marble.
ROBOT WIRING

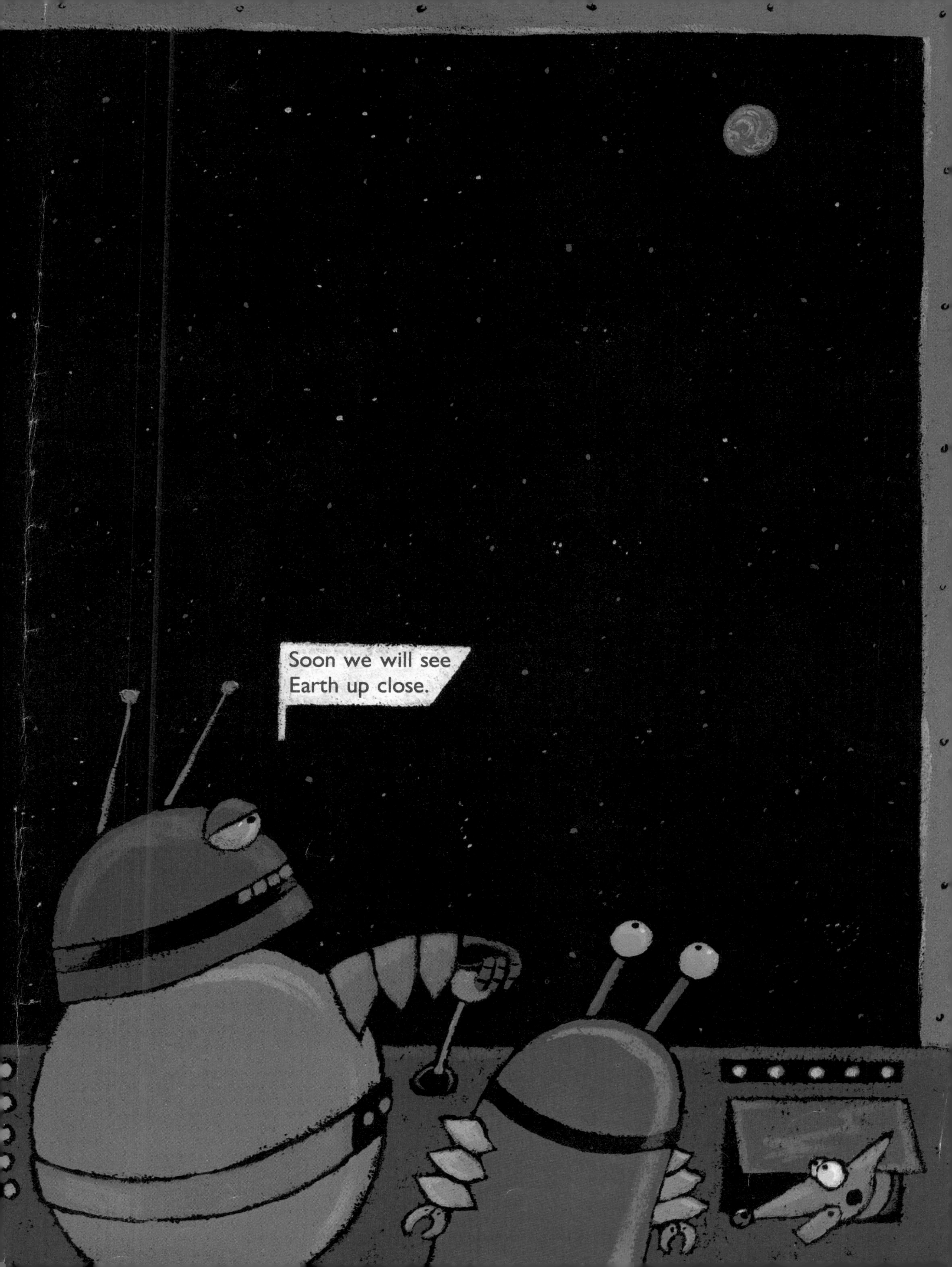
Soon we will see Earth up close.

Look at all that water!
The earth's surface is about 70% water and 30% land.
The large areas of water are oceans.
The large land masses are continents.

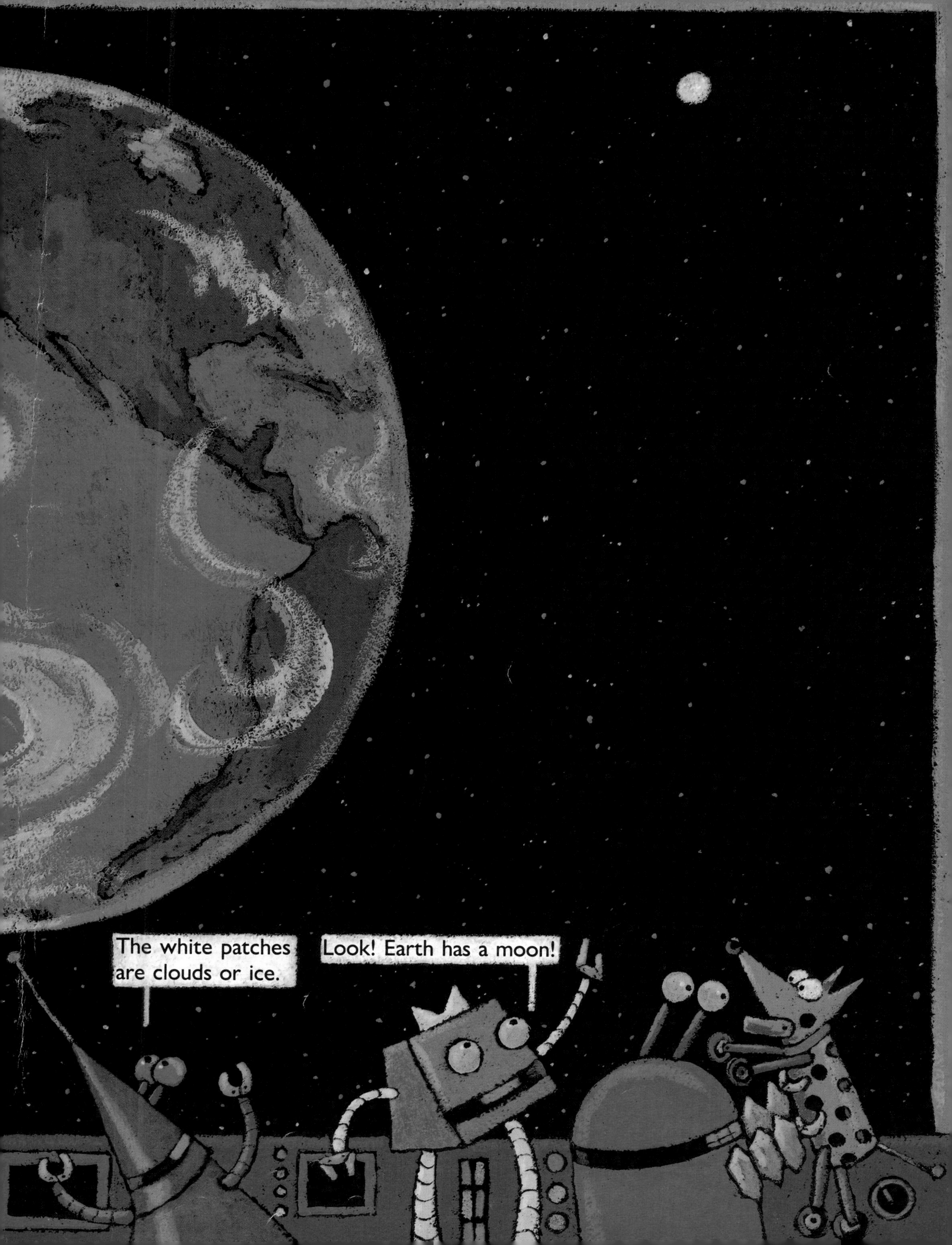
The white patches are clouds or ice.
Look! Earth has a moon!

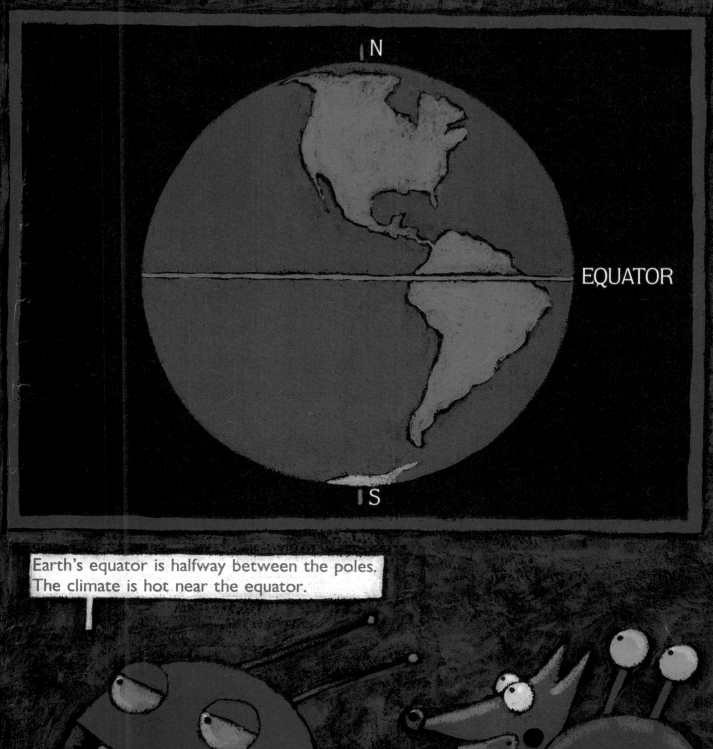

N

EQUATOR

S

Earth's equator is halfway between the poles.
The climate is hot near the equator.

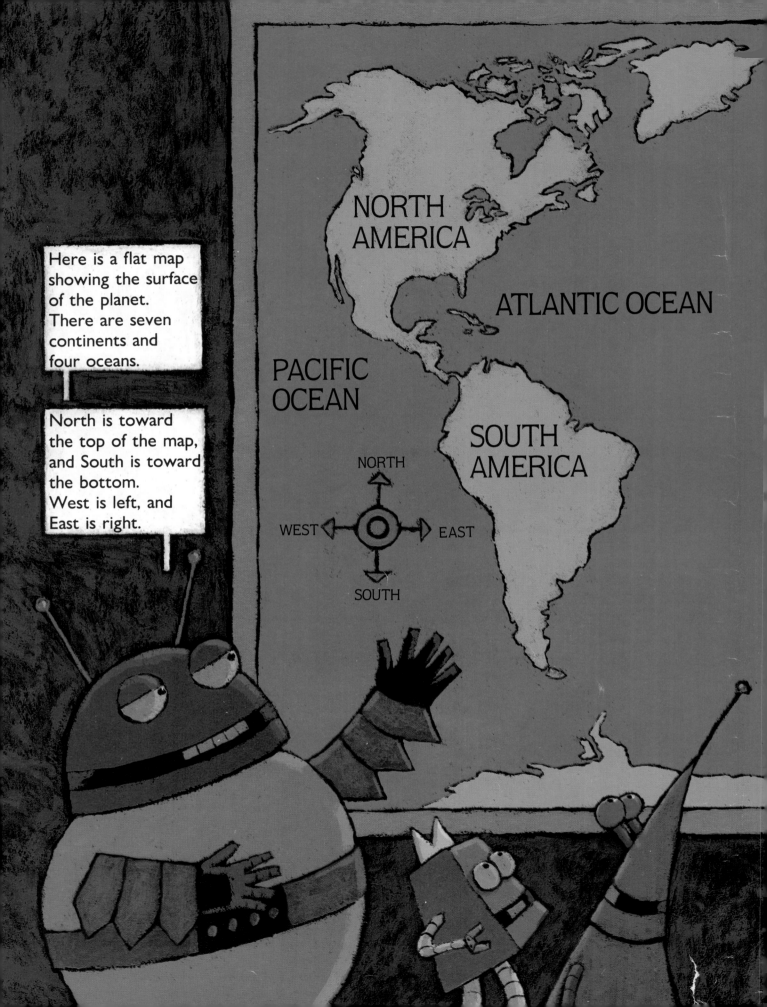

Here is a flat map showing the surface of the planet. There are seven continents and four oceans.

North is toward the top of the map, and South is toward the bottom. West is left, and East is right.

NORTH AMERICA

ATLANTIC OCEAN

PACIFIC OCEAN

SOUTH AMERICA

NORTH

WEST

EAST

SOUTH

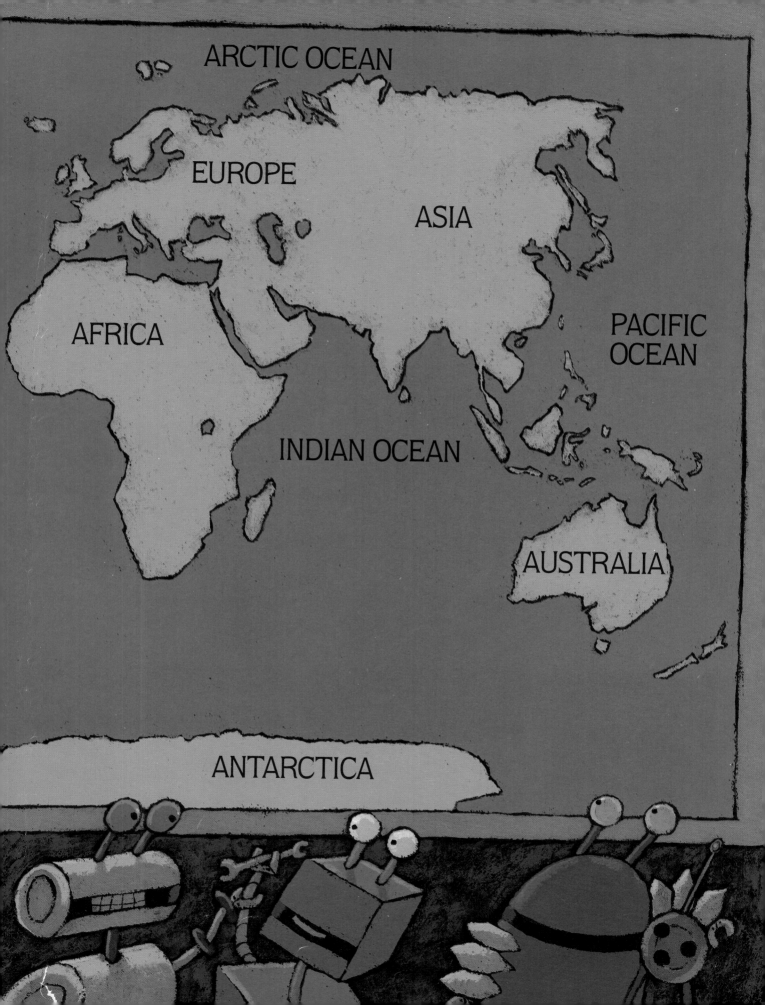

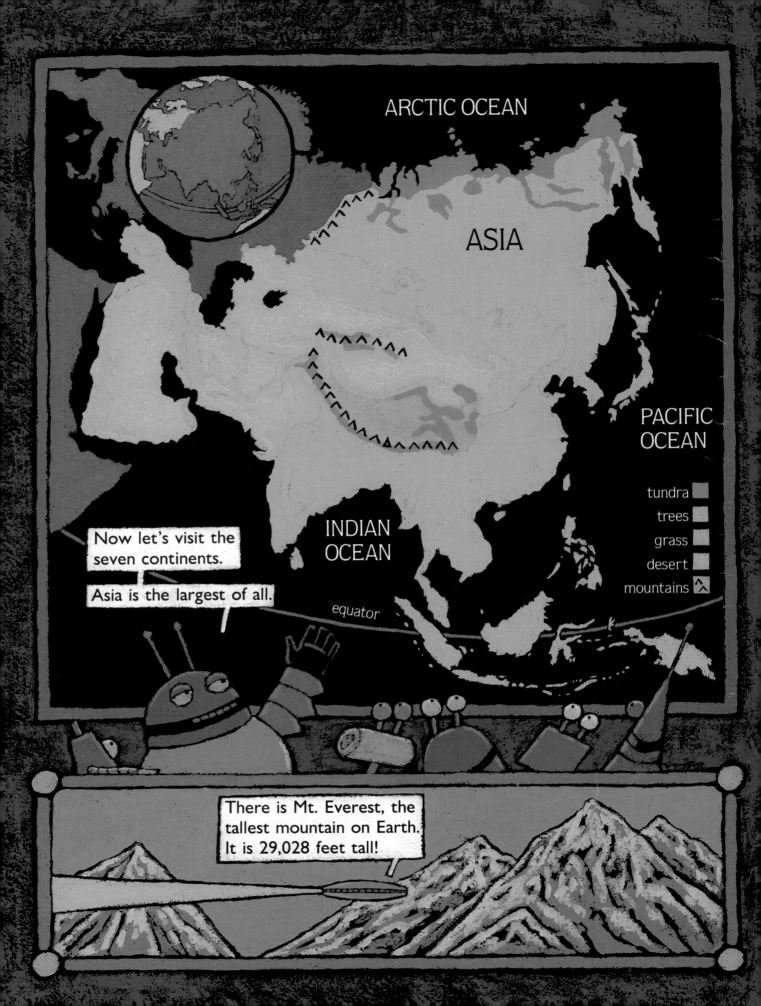

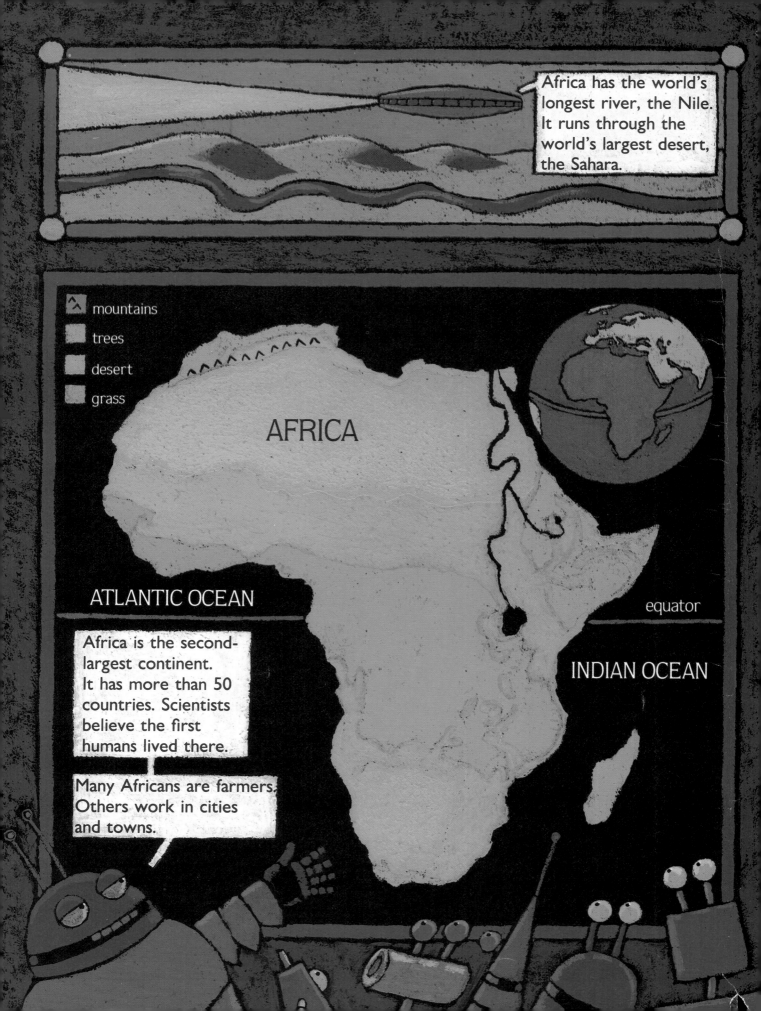

Africa has the world's longest river, the Nile. It runs through the world's largest desert, the Sahara.

mountains
trees
desert
grass

AFRICA

ATLANTIC OCEAN

equator

INDIAN OCEAN

Africa is the second-largest continent. It has more than 50 countries. Scientists believe the first humans lived there.

Many Africans are farmers. Others work in cities and towns.

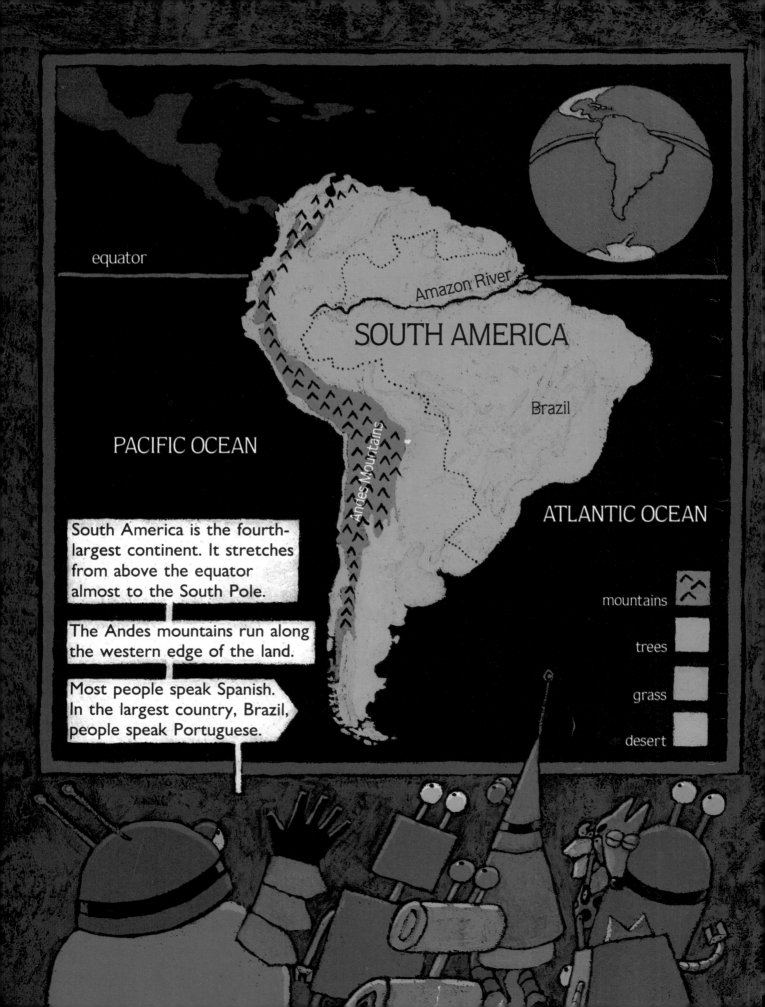

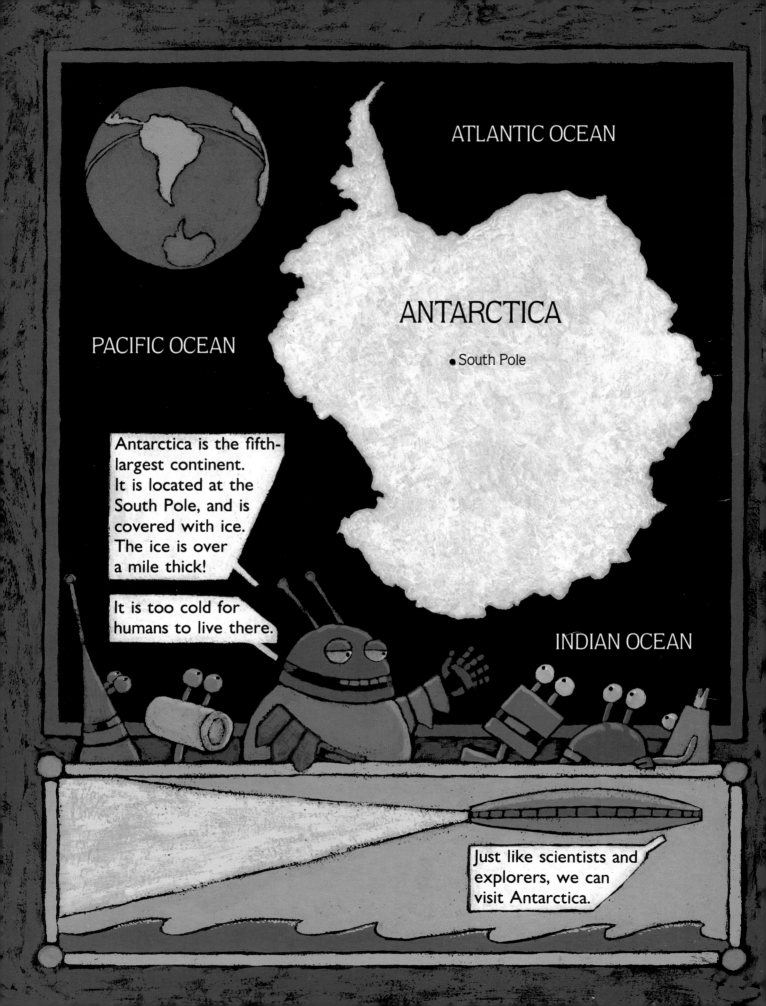

All aboard! We are leaving Earth now!
Awwwwww! Do we have to, Mr. Quark?
Yes. But we can come back again on another field trip.

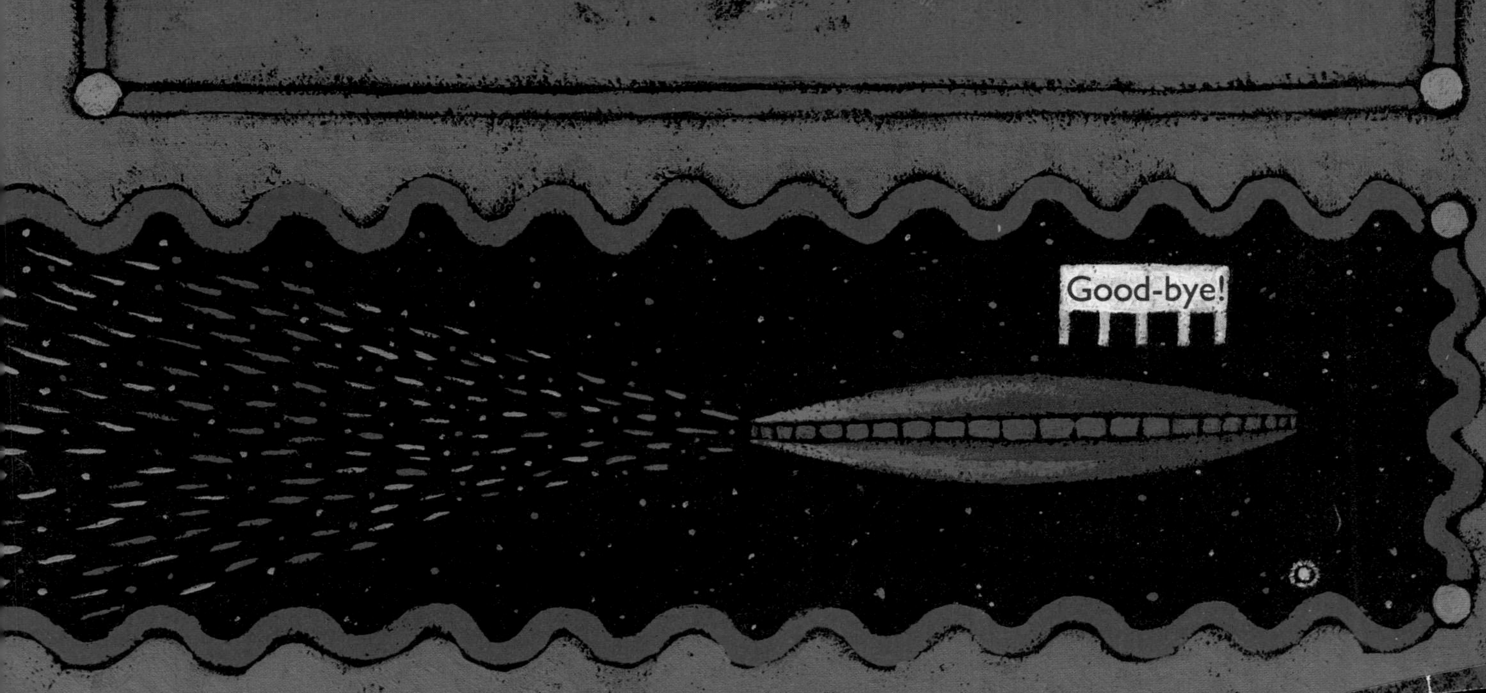
Good-bye!

OUR TRIP TO EARTH

THE GREAT WALL OF CHINA IN ASIA

THE PYRAMIDS IN AFRICA

REDWOOD FOREST IN NORTH AMERICA

INCAN RUINS IN SOUTH AMERICA

SNOW SCULPTURE IN ANTARCTICA

SKIING IN THE ALPS IN EUROPE

THE GREAT BARRIER REEF IN AUSTRALIA

THE EARTH — A BEAUTIFUL PLANET!